Christ-Centered Thanksgiving

Great Waters Press
Making Biblical Family Life Practical

©2011 Hal & Melanie Young, All Rights Reserved
Great Waters Press
www.GreatWatersPress.com

This eBook is not licensed for resale. This license is personal to the original purchaser and may not be sold, loaned, or otherwise transferred to third parties or additional users. Purchaser may make one copy for each member of their immediate household. Additional Licenses should be purchased if you'd like to share this eBook with anyone outside your family. Contact info@greatwaterspress.com for information.

Copying for school or co-op use is strictly prohibited. Each student should purchase their own copy.

No part of this publication may otherwise be published, reproduced, stored in a retrieval system, or transmitted or copied in any form or by any means now known or hereafter developed, whether electronic, mechanical, or otherwise, without prior written permission of the publisher. Illegal use, copying, publication, transfer or distribution is considered copyright infringement according to Sections 107 and 108 and other relevant portions of the United States Copyright Act.

Readers should be aware that Internet Web sites offered as sources for further information may have changed or disappeared between the time this was written and when it is read.

The use of Facebook™, Twitter™, or any other trademarked names does not imply endorsement or approval by the companies holding those trademarks. This document is intended only to enhance your user experience.

Scripture quotations are from the Holy Bible, English Standard Version, copyright © 2001, 2007 by Crossway Bibles, a division of Good News Publishers. Used by permission. All rights reserved.

Table of Contents

Introduction

    Grasping the Opportunity   5
    Why do We Celebrate?   6
    Who were the Pilgrims, and why are they important?   6

Readings from History and Literature
    The Foundation of our Celebration   9
    Gov. William Bradford, *Of Plimoth Plantation*   9
    Edward Winslow et al., *Mourt's Relation, or The Journal of the Plantation at Plymouth*   15
    "Five Kernels of Corn"   18
    "Forefathers' Song"   20
    George Washington's General Thanksgiving Proclamation   22
    Abraham Lincoln's Proclamation of Thanksgiving   24
    The Thanksgiving Tree   26

Songs of Thanksgiving
    What did the Pilgrims Sing?   27
    All People That on Earth Do Dwell   27
    We Gather Together   29
    Come, Ye Thankful People, Come   31
    Now Thank We All Our God   32

The Thanksgiving Feast
    Menu   33
    Becoming a Great Cook   34
    How to Roast a Turkey   36
    Next Day Turkey Gumbo   40
    Cornbread Dressing   41
    Grandma's Cranberry Relish   42
    Fresh Cranberry Sauce   43

Savory Turkey Gravy	43
Creamed or Mashed Potatoes	44
Rice	45
Seven Layer Salad	46
Congealed Salad	47
Macaroni and Cheese Pie	48
Sweet Potato Souffle	50
Green Bean Casserole	51
Garden Vegetables	51
Homemade Buttermilk Biscuits	52
Chocolate Meringue Pie	53
Pumpkin Cheesecake Pie	55

Cooking Schedule

The Shopping List	57
In Advance	59
Tuesday or Wednesday Before Thanksgiving	59
Thanksgiving Day	60

The Feast

An Order of Events	62
Songs of Thanksgiving Sheet	63
Cooking Schedule Forms	64

Other Great Resources	66
Acknowledgements	70

Introduction

Grasping the Opportunity

Thanksgiving is one of the least commercialized and altered holidays of our time. Though for many people, it has become merely "Turkey Day," the name and the Pilgrim traditions surrounding it remind even the calloused to remember the God who made us and takes care of us.

This gives you a tremendous opportunity to be a testimony to your extended family! By introducing Christ-centered traditions and focusing on the meaning of the holiday, you can witness to your family in a very low key, winsome way and hosting the celebration at your house allows you to set the tone in a way you just can't at someone else's house.

You're probably thinking that cooking for Thanksgiving is a tremendous lot of work, but it is so worth it when you realize the opportunity you have to glorify the Lord in it! That hard work may be the factor that makes older relatives willing to pass on the baton, too.

Be sure to ask other family members to help, though, not just to lessen your own burden, but to make everyone feel appreciated and to allow them to contribute, as well. "Nana, you'll please, please, please bring your cornbread dressing like we always have, won't you?" Or, "Aunt Beth, could you make the seven layer salad? No one does it like you do!"

We've found that as we've introduced some new/old traditions to our Feast, that actually our extended family has welcomed and enjoyed them. We'll never forget a dear relative filming our son reciting "Five Kernels of Corn" so that he could take it back to show his friends in China!

Grasp this opportunity to help everyone remember what Thanksgiving is all about!

Why do we celebrate?

There is not one of us who has not sinned against God. Jesus said that if we lust in our hearts, we have committed adultery. If that is so, and it is, there is no one alive who is not a liar, a thief, an adulterer and worse at heart.

As sinners, we are tragically and completely unable to reconcile ourselves to God through good works. Isaiah says, "all our righteous deeds are like a polluted garment," and Romans, "The wages of sin is death." We are condemned by God's holiness and justice, but He has not left us in that condition! Jesus said, "Fear not, little flock, for it is your Father's good pleasure to give you the kingdom.

He sent His son Jesus Christ to die in our place. That verse in Romans 6:23 continues, "but the free gift of God is eternal life in Christ Jesus our Lord." What a blessing that what we would earn and cannot is given to us as a free gift!

"For by grace you have been saved through faith. And this is not your own doing; it is the gift of God,[9] not a result of works, so that no one may boast." Ephesians 2:8-9

So, when we have repented of our sins and trusted Him to save us, we have every reason in the world, every reason in all of the universe to be full of Thanksgiving, no matter what happens otherwise.

Recognizing that every good and perfect gift comes from God changes our whole perspective on life. Suddenly we realize that the check that came just in time, was God's provision. We see that the friends that came to help when the baby was in the hospital are showing us God's love. We begin to see that every lovely sight, every moment of joy, every happy sound, every good thing, is a gift from our Father in Heaven and is a reason for Thanksgiving.

Who were the Pilgrims?

When a small group of Christian families set out a tiny English colony on the shores of Cape Cod, Massachusetts, in 1621, they not only founded a new sort of nation, but a new way of thinking about freedom.

The Reformation, started a hundred years before in Germany by a Catholic priest named Martin Luther, had swept northern Europe, but it was slow coming to

England. While King Henry VIII had split the English church from the Church of Rome, setting an archbishop he controlled to lead the new church in place of the Pope, it was not a sweeping change of teaching and faith. That came later, as groups within the new Church of England sought to introduce more biblical teaching about faith, salvation, and good works. This group, which became known as Puritans for their emphasis on pure scriptural teaching and living, tried to reform the English church from within.

Others considered it was better to start over with an entirely separate church. These so-called Separatists found themselves in trouble with both the established church and even the King himself, because their claim to have freedom of conscience placed them out of control of both Church and Crown—or so it was thought. For years, these small groups were threatened with punishments ranging from fines for not attending services of the Church of England, to imprisonment and confiscation of homes, businesses, and all other goods, and in some cases, even death. All the while these believers and their pastors proclaimed loyalty to the king and obedience to all other laws.

Finally, in 1608, a number of families escaped to Holland, where they hoped to have freedom from persecution and have the ability to worship God and raise their families without fear of attack. For several years they lived and worked in Holland, settling near the city of Leyden. Unfortunately, their strong work ethic made their Dutch neighbors resentful of their success, and the temptations of the nearby cities began to draw away their children from their parents' and pastors' spiritual leadership.

In 1620, then, a group of Separatists (now called "Pilgrims" for their "wandering" from England to Holland) decided to leave Leyden and establish a new colony on the coast of Virginia, a vast territory claimed by England along the American coastline. An earlier settlement at Roanoke Island had vanished, but one begun in 1607 at Jamestown was growing, and the Pilgrims considered a new community founded by themselves would allow them to make laws and customs which would support and encourage Christian life as they believed God expected.

With the financial backing of investors in England who were anxious to profit from the un-touched timber and other resources of the New World, the Pilgrims purchased two ships, the *Mayflower* and the small *Speedwell*. After many delays and sending *Speedwell* back for repairs, the *Mayflower* set out from Plymouth, England in early September 1620.

Crossing the Atlantic in a tiny sailing ship was dangerous in the best weather, and the delays meant the *Mayflower* was sailing through the start of the stormy season. The ship was badly damaged at one point, and the Pilgrims used some of their own tools and supplies to help repair the vessel. Their calm acceptance of discomfort, rough sailing, and even verbal abuse by the sailors, was a testimony to the crew of their faith in God and submission to His will.

Finally the *Mayflower* made the coast of what is now called Massachusetts, and the captain refused to take any longer to travel southward, closer to the Jamestown settlement. Instead, the Pilgrims would be put ashore at a deserted natural harbor along Cape Cod. This settlement would be named Plymouth, after their last look at British soil.

Why are the Pilgrims important?

The Pilgrims are the spiritual and governmental forefathers of our country, and particularly, the Christians among our countrymen. Though the Jamestown colony was earlier than Plymouth, it would be the principles and laws of Plymouth that would form the basis for what our country would become – the freest on earth. Our heritage of religious freedom comes directly from them. It would be their vision that most influenced our nation.

Our Thanksgiving celebration flows out of their history. Let's learn more, in their own words:

Readings from History and Literature

The Foundation of Our Celebration

William Bradford was one of the early leaders of the Plymouth settlement, serving as its second governor after the death of the first governor, John Carver, and one of its earliest historians. His book, *Of Plimoth Plantation*, includes his description of the arrival of the Pilgrims and their agreement we know as "The Mayflower Compact." Here he describes the conflict that led to their covenant:

> I shall a little return back and begin with a combination made by them before they came ashore, being the first foundation of their government in this place; occasioned partly by the discontented and mutinous speeches that some of the strangers amongst them had let fall from them in the ship—That when they came ashore they would use their own liberty; for none had the power to command them, the patent they had being for Virginia, and not for New England, which belonged to another Government, with which the Virginia Company had nothing to do. And partly that such an act by

them done (this their condition considered) might be as firm as any patent, and in some respects more sure.[1]

Although the Pilgrims were leaving England because of the religious oppression they had experienced at home, and were relocating to America in hope of establishing a colony where they could practice their faith without fear or interference, not everyone on board the *Mayflower* was a Pilgrim. These outsiders, called "strangers," were a source of friction and trouble through the early years. Here, they threatened to ignore the leadership of the Plymouth community on the grounds that they had actually landed in New England rather than Virginia, as intended. To ensure an understanding of the form of government they would create, the Pilgrims entered into the *Mayflower Compact:*

> In the name of God, Amen. We whose names are underwritten, the loyal subjects of our dread sovereign Lord, King James, by the grace of God, of Great Britain, France, and Ireland king, defender of the faith, etc., having undertaken, for the glory of God, and the advancement of the Christian faith, and honour of our king and country, a voyage to plant the first colony in the Northern parts of Virginia, do by these presents solemnly and mutually in the presence of God, and of one another, covenant and combine ourselves together into a civil body politic, for our better ordering and preservation and furtherance of the ends aforesaid; and by virtue hereof to enact, constitute, and frame such just and equal laws, ordinances, acts, constitutions, and offices, from time to time, as shall be thought most meet and convenient for the general good of the Colony, unto which we promise all due submission and obedience. In witness whereof we have hereunder subscribed our names at Cape Cod the eleventh of November, in the year of the reign of our sovereign lord, King James, of England, France, and Ireland the eighteenth, and of Scotland the fifty-fourth. Anno Domini 1620.[2]

This clearly declared their loyalty to the King of England, but also, their **intent to settle for the glory of God and advancement of His kingdom.** The colony would be an organized community under a consensual government, and not merely a cluster of independent households which just happened to be near one another.

---

[1] William Bradford, *Of Plimouth Plantation*, p. 109 (page numbers refer to the original manuscript). I have modernized the spelling and punctuation and expanded archaic abbreviations for easier reading (for example, "y^e Govr" becomes "the Governor")
[2] Bradford, p. 110.

Signing of the Mayflower Compact

Jesus said that "By this all men will know that you are my disciples, if you love one another."[3] The Pilgrims found their time to demonstrate that character came very soon:

> In these hard and difficult beginnings they found some discontents and murmurings arise amongst some, and mutinous speeches and carriages in other; but they were soon quelled and overcome by the wisdom, patience, and just and equal carriage of things by the Governor and better part, which clave faithfully together in the main. But that which was most sad and lamentable was, that in two or three months' time half of their company died, especially in January and February, being the depth of winter, and wanting houses and other comforts; being infected with the scurvy and other diseases, which this long voyage and their inaccommodate condition had brought upon them; so as there died sometimes two or three of a day, in the foresaid time; that of 100 and odd persons, scarce 50 remained. And of these in the time of most distress, there was but six or seven sound persons, who, to their great commendations be it spoken, spared no pains, night nor day, but with abundance of toil and hazard of their own health,

---

[3] John 13:35 (ESV)

fetch them wood, made them fires, dressed them meat, made their beds, washed their loathsome clothes, clothed and unclothed them; in a word, did all the homely and necessary offices for them which dainty and queasy stomachs cannot endure to hear named; and all this willingly and cheerfully, without any grudging in the least, showing herein their true love unto their friend and brethren. A rare example and worthy to be remembered. ... And yet the Lord so upheld these persons, as in this general calamity they were not at all infected either with sickness, or lameness. And what I have said of these, I may say of many others who died in this general visitation, and others yet living, that whilst they had health, yea, or any strength continuing, they were not wanting to any that had need of them. And I doubt not but their recompense is with the Lord.[4]

The Old Fort and First Meeting House

Bradford marveled at the contrast between their community and the worldliness of the sailors and strangers which had followed them:

But I may not here pass by another remarkable passage not to be forgotten. As this calamity fell among the passengers that were to be left here to plant ...the disease began to fall amongst them [the ship's crew] also, so as almost half their company died before they went away, and many of their officers and lustiest men, as the bos'un, gunner, three quartermasters, the cook, and others. At which the master was something stricken and sent to the sick ashore and told the Governor he should send for beer for them that had need of it, though he drunk water homeward bound. But now amongst his company there was far another kind of carriage in this misery than amongst

---

[4] Bradford, pp. 111-112,

the passengers; for they that before had been boon companions in drinking and jollity in the time of their health and welfare, began now to desert one another in this calamity, saying they would not hazard their lives for them, they should be infected by coming to help them in their cabins, and so, after they came to die by it, would do little or nothing for them, but if they died let them die. But such of the passengers as were yet aboard showed them what mercy they could, which made some of their hearts relent, as the bos'un (and some others), who was a proud young man, and would often curse and scoff at the passengers; but when he grew weak, they had compassion on him and helped him; then he confessed he did not deserve it at their hands, he had abused them in word and deed. "O!" saith he, "you, I now see, show your love like Christians indeed to one another, but we let one another lie and die like dogs." Another lay cursing his wife, saying if it had been for her he had never come this unlucky voyage, and one cursing his fellows, saying he had done this and that, for some of them, he had spent so much and so much, amongst them, and they were now weary of him, and did not help him, having need. Another gave his companion all he had, if he died, to help him in his weakness; he went and got a little spice and made him a mess of meat once or twice, and because he died not so soon as he expected, he went amongst his fellows, and swore the rogue would cousin him, he would see him choked before he made him any more meat; and yet the poor fellow died before morning.[5]

As winter turned to spring, the survivors began to cultivate their fields—and an unexpected friendship:

All this while the Indians came skulking about them, and would sometimes show themselves aloof of, but when any approached near them, they would run away. And once they stole away their tools where they had been at work, and were gone to dinner. But about the 16th of March a certain Indian came boldly amongst them, and spoke to them in broken English, which they could well understand, but marveled at it. At length they understood by discourse with him, that he was not of these parts, but belonged to the eastern parts, where some English ships came to fish, with whom he was acquainted, and could name sundry of them by their names, amongst whom he had got his language. He became profitable to them in acquainting them with many things concerning the state of the country in the east-parts where he lived, which was afterwards profitable unto them; as also of the

---

[5] Bradford, pp. 112-114.

people here, of their names, number, and strength; of their situation and distance from this place, and who was chief amongst them. His name was **Samoset**; he told them also of another Indian whose name was **Squanto**, a native of this place, who had been in England and could speak better English than himself.[6]

Several days after this remarkable meeting, the nearby chief **Massasoit** paid a visit, accompanied by Squanto. After a peace treaty was negotiated, the chief departed but left Squanto with the Pilgrims:

> *Squanto* continued with them, and was their interpreter, and was a special instrument sent of God for their good beyond their expectation. He directed them how to set their corn, where to take fish, and to procure other commodities, and was also their pilot to bring them to unknown places for their profit, and never left them until he died.[7]

After a difficult growing season, sometime in late September or October, the Pilgrims prepared their first harvest

> They began now to gather in the small harvest they had, and to fit up their houses and dwellings against winter, being all well recovered in health and strength, and had all things in good plenty; for as some were thus employed in affairs abroad, others were exercised in fishing, about cod, and bass, and other fish, of which they took good store, of which every family had their portion. All the summer there was no want. And now began to come in store of fowl, as winter approached, of which this place did abound when they came first (but afterward decreased by degrees). And besides waterfowl, there was great store of wild turkeys, of which they took many, besides venison, etc. Besides they had about a peck of meal a week to a person, or now since harvest, Indian corn to the proportion. Which made many afterwards write so largely of their plenty to their friends in England, which were not feigned, but true reports.

---

[6] Bradford, pp. 114-115.
[7] Bradford, p. 116.

E dward Winslow (who succeeded Bradford as the third governor) along with Bradford and other men of the colony contributed to a book known as *Mourt's Relation, or, The Journal of the Plantation at Plymouth*. ("Mourt" is thought to be George Morton, who wrote an introduction to the book when it was first published. He was not one of the Pilgrims himself.) This passage, where he describes for a friend the situation at Plymouth, was sent in December 1621 when the Pilgrims had been in New England just thirteen months.

> Loving, and old Friend, although I received no Letter from you by this Ship, yet forasmuch as I know you expect the performance of my promise, which was, to write unto you truly and faithfully of all things, I have therefore at this time sent to you accordingly. Referring you for further satisfaction to our more large Relations [i.e., the rest of the book]. You shall understand, that in this little time, that a few of us have been here, we have built seven dwelling houses, and four for the use of the Plantation, and have made preparations for divers others. We set the last Spring some twenty Acres of *Indian* Corn, and sowed some six Acres of Barley and Peas, and according to the manner of the *Indians*, we manured our ground with Herrings or rather Shad, which have in great abundance, and take with great ease at our doors. Our Corn did prove well, and God be praised, we had a good increase of *Indian*-Corn, and our Barley indifferent good, but our Peas not worth the

gathering, for we feared they were too late sown, they came up very well, and blossomed, but the Sun parched them in the blossom;

And then he described the **first thanksgiving celebration:**

> ... our harvest being gotten in, our Governor sent four men on fowling, that so we might after a more special manner rejoice together, after we had gathered the fruit of our labors; they four in one day killed as much fowl, as with a little help beside, served the Company almost a week, at which time amongst other Recreations, we exercised our Arms [i.e., held shooting competitions], many of the Indians coming amongst us, and amongst the rest their greatest King Massasoit, with some ninety men, whom for three days we entertained and feasted, and they went out and killed five Deer, which they brought to the Plantation and bestowed on our Governor, and upon the Captain, and others. And although it be not always so plentiful, as it was at this time with us, yet by the goodness of God, we are so far from want, that we often with you partakers of our plenty.[8]

There were still times of difficulty and famine ahead, even in the months immediately after Winslow's letter, but the Pilgrims plainly saw the providential care of God in their success making a living out of the wilderness of Cape Cod the very first year. And now, even when we face uncertainty at our year's end, we too should reflect—and rejoice—over God's love and provision for His people for all times.

Further Reading:

William Bradford, *Of Plimoth Plantation.*
RaisingRealMen.com/Bradford

Edward Winslow, *Mourt's Relation, or the Journal of the Plantation at Plymouth.*
RaisingRealMen.com/Winslow

Pilgrim Hall Museum, Plymouth, Mass.
http://www.pilgrimhall.org/

---

[8] Edward Winslow, *Mourt's Relation*, pp. 60-61 in the original

Interested in what happened afterward? In the following years the Pilgrims spread inland and along the coast, and in 1628, the Massachusetts Bay Colony and the town of Boston were founded by the Puritans, a group with similar beliefs which had chosen to remain within the Church of England.

The original Plymouth Colony was founded with the aid of the Native Americans of the area, particularly Squanto and Massosoit. Massosoit's son, Metacom, or King Phillip, however, distrusted the Europeans and a breakdown in relations and respect led to his destruction of Swansea, a town of the colonists. The disastrous King Philip's War which resulted in 1675-6 took a terrible toll in life and wealth on both sides. The Indian population retreated further inland, while the expansion of the English colony was set back a generation. The recent book *Mayflower* by Nathaniel Philbrick recounts the history from the Plymouth landing to the conclusion of that conflict, and shows the power of honesty, respect, and trust, and the high cost of losing them.

Five Kernels of Corn

by Hezekiah Butterworth

'Twas the year of the famine in Plymouth of old,
The ice and the snow from the thatched roofs had rolled;
Through the warm purple skies steered the geese o'er the seas,
And the woodpeckers tapped in the clocks of the trees;
And the boughs on the slopes to the south winds lay bare,
and dreaming of summer, the buds swelled in the air.
The pale Pilgrims welcomed each reddening morn;
There were left but for rations Five Kernels of Corn.
Five Kernels of Corn!
Five Kernels of Corn!
But to Bradford a feast were Five Kernels of Corn!

"Five Kernels of Corn! Five Kernels of Corn!
Ye people, be glad for Five Kernels of Corn!"
So Bradford cried out on bleak Burial Hill,
And the thin women stood in their doors, white and still.
"Lo, the harbor of Plymouth rolls bright in the Spring,
The maples grow red, and the wood robins sing,
The west wind is blowing, and fading the snow,
And the pleasant pines sing, and arbutuses blow.
Five Kernels of Corn!
Five Kernels of Corn!
To each one be given Five Kernels of Corn!"

O Bradford of Austerfield hast on thy way,
The west winds are blowing o'er Provincetown Bay,
The white avens bloom, but the pine domes are chill,
And new graves have furrowed Precisioners' Hill!
"Give thanks, all ye people, the warm skies have come,
The hilltops are sunny, and green grows the holm,
And the trumpets of winds, and the white March is gone,
Five Kernels of Corn!
Five Kernels of Corn!
Ye have for Thanksgiving Five Kernels of Corn!

"The raven's gift eat and be humble and pray,
A new light is breaking and Truth leads your way;
One taper a thousand shall kindle; rejoice
That to you has been given the wilderness voice!"
O Bradford of Austerfield, daring the wave,
And safe through the sounding blasts leading the brave,
Of deeds such as thine was the free nation born,
And the festal world sings the "Five Kernels of Corn."
Five Kernels of Corn!
Five Kernels of Corn!
The nation gives thanks for Five Kernels of Corn!
To the Thanksgiving Feast bring Five Kernels of Corn!

The Forefathers' Song

*Although said to have been written in 1630, it was not recorded in writing until well over 100 years later.
Written in a humorous vein, it does illustrate the challenges of being a colonist.
The memorable pumpkin section has been quoted by schoolchildren for nearly 200 years!*

New England's annoyances you that would know them,
Pray ponder these verses which briefly doth show them.
The place where we live is a wilderness wood,
Where grass is much wanting that's fruitful and good:
Our mountains and hills and our valley below,
Being commonly covered with ice and with snow;
And when the north-west wind with violence blows,
Then every man pulls his cap over his nose:
But if any's so hardy and will it withstand,
He forfeits a finger, a foot or a hand.

But when the Spring opens we then take the hoe,
And make the ground ready to plant and to sow;
Our corn being planted and seed being sown,
The worms destroy much before it is grown;
And when it is growing, some spoil there is made
By birds and by squirrels that pluck up the blade;
And when it is come to full corn in the ear,
It is often destroyed by raccoon and by deer.

And now our garments begin to grow thin,
And wool is much wanted to card and to spin;
If we can get a garment to cover without,
Our other in-garments are clout upon clout:
Our clothes we brought with us are apt to be torn,
They need to be clouted soon after they're worn,
But clouting our garments they hinder us nothing,
Clouts double are warmer than single whole clothing.

If fresh meat be wanting to fill up our dish,
We have carrots and turnips as much as we wish:
And if there's a mind for a delicate dish
We repair to the clam-banks, and there we catch fish.
Instead of pottage and puddings and custards and pies,
Our pumpkins and parsnips are common supplies;
We have pumpkins at morning and pumpkins at noon,
If it was not for pumpkins we should [all] be undone! ["undoon", perhaps]

If barley be wanting to make into malt,
We must be contented, and think it no fault;
For we can make liquor to sweeten our lips,
Of pumpkins and parsnips and walnut-tree chips.
Now while some are going let others be coming,
For while liquor's boiling, it must have a scumming;
But I will not blame them, for birds of a feather,
By seeking their fellows are flocking together.

But you whom the Lord intends hither to bring,
Forsake not the honey for fear of the sting;
But bring both a quiet and contented mind,
And all needful blessings you surely will find.

General Thanksgiving

By the PRESIDENT of the United States Of America
A PROCLAMATION

WHEREAS it is the duty of all nations to acknowledge the providence of Almighty God, to obey His will, to be grateful for His benefits, and humbly to implore His protection and favour; and Whereas both Houses of Congress have, by their joint committee, requested me "to recommend to the people of the United States a DAY OF PUBLICK THANKSGIVING and PRAYER, to be observed by acknowledging with grateful hearts the many and signal favors of Almighty God, especially by affording them an opportunity peaceably to establish a form of government for their safety and happiness:

NOW THEREFORE, I do recommend and assign THURSDAY, the TWENTY-SIXTH DAY of NOVEMBER next, to be devoted by the people of these States to the service of that great and glorious Being who is the beneficent author of all the good that was, that is, or that will be; that we may then all unite in rendering unto Him our sincere and humble thanks for His kind care and protection of the people of this country previous to their becoming a nation; for the signal and manifold mercies and the favorable interpositions of His providence in the course and conclusion of the late war; for the great degree of tranquility, union, and plenty which we have since enjoyed;-- for the peaceable and rational manner in which we have been enable to establish Constitutions of government for our safety and happiness, and particularly the national one now lately instituted;-- for the civil and religious liberty with which we are blessed, and the means we have of acquiring and diffusing useful knowledge;-- and, in general, for all the great and various favours which He has been pleased to confer upon us.

And also, that we may then unite in most humbly offering our prayers and supplications to the great Lord and Ruler of Nations and beseech Him to pardon our national and other transgressions;-- to enable us all, whether in publick or private stations, to perform our several and relative duties properly and punctually; to render our National Government a blessing to all the people by constantly being a Government of wife, just, and constitutional laws, discreetly and faithfully executed and obeyed; to protect and guide all sovereigns and nations (especially such as have shewn kindness unto us); and to bless them with good governments, peace, and concord; to promote the knowledge and practice of true religion and virtue, and the increase of science among them and us; and, generally to grant unto all mankind such a degree of temporal prosperity as he alone knows to be best.

GIVEN under my hand, at the city of New-York, the third day of October, in the year of our Lord, one thousand seven hundred and eighty-nine.

(signed) G. Washington

Washington Resigns His Military Commission,

Leading the Way for a Government of Laws, not Men, nor Power

Proclamation of Thanksgiving
by the President of the United States of America

The year that is drawing toward its close has been filled with the blessings of fruitful years and healthful skies. To these bounties, which are so constantly enjoyed that we are prone to forget the Source from which they come, others have been added which are of so extraordinary a nature that they can not fail to penetrate and soften even the heart which is habitually insensible to the ever-watchful providence of Almighty God.

In the midst of a civil war of unequaled magnitude and severity, which has sometimes seemed to foreign states to invite and to provoke their aggression, peace has been preserved with all nations, order has been maintained, the laws have been respected and obeyed, and harmony has prevailed everywhere, except in the theater of military conflict, while that theater has been greatly contracted by the advancing armies and navies of the Union.

Needful diversions of wealth and of strength from the field of peaceful industry to the national defense have not arrested the plow, the shuttle, or the ship; the ax has enlarged the borders of our settlements, and the mines, as well of iron and coal as of the precious metals, have yielded even more abundantly than theretofore. Population has steadily increased notwithstanding the waste that has been made in the camp, the siege, and the battlefield, and the country, rejoicing in the consciousness of augmented strength and vigor, is permitted to expect continuance of years with large increase of freedom.

No human counsel hath devised nor hath any mortal hand worked out these great things. They are the gracious gifts of the Most High God, who, while dealing with us in anger for our sins, hath nevertheless remembered mercy.

It has seemed to me fit and proper that they should be solemnly, reverently, and gratefully acknowledged, as with one heart and one voice, by the whole American people. I do therefore invite my fellow-citizens in every part of the United States, and also those who are at sea and those who are sojourning in foreign lands, to set apart and observe the last Thursday of November next as a day of thanksgiving and praise to our beneficent Father who dwelleth in the heavens. And I recommend to them that while offering up the ascriptions justly due to Him for such singular deliverances and blessings they do also, with humble penitence for our national perverseness and disobedience, commend to His tender care all those who have become widows, orphans, mourners, or sufferers in the lamentable civil strife in which we are unavoidably engaged, and fervently implore the interposition of the Almighty Hand to heal the wounds of the nation and to restore it, as soon as may be consistent with the Divine purposes, to the full enjoyment of peace, harmony, tranquility, and union.

In testimony wherof I have herunto set my hand and caused the seal of the United States to be affixed.

[Signed]
A. Lincoln

The Thanksgiving Tree

Many years ago, Hal was told that his company was downsizing and his job was being eliminated. While we had some time to wrap things up before the paycheck ended, there was still a lot of uncertainty and concern in our family—and this happened just at the start of November, leading into the holidays.

To help us focus on what we knew was most important, Hal brought home a roll of brown paper and drew a simple, branching tree trunk, like the oak trees that lined the streets of our town. He fastened this to the wall in the kitchen where we ate all our meals, then brought in a fallen leaf, a stack of construction paper, and a pair of scissors. Using the leaf as a pattern, we cut a large stack of yellow, orange, red, and a few green paper leaves.

Every time we sat down, we took a marker and wrote down things we were thankful for, then taped them to the branches of the tree on the wall. The obvious things went up first—thankful for each other, our health, a home to live in—but soon we had to start really thinking. Where had God blessed us and we took it for granted? We discovered we were thankful for the ability to read. We were thankful for the Bible. We praised God for eyeglasses. Hal and Melanie being science-minded people, they were thankful for repeatable experiments. We remembered that many countries don't have reliable clean water, so we put "clean water" on the tree, too. What sounded like a joke when we first thought of it, often became a moment of insight, that we were surrounded by a thousand pleasant and providential things which we never noticed from day to day.

By the time Thanksgiving rolled around, we had covered the tree and started creating "piles" of leaves at the bottom of the trunk. We had fun showing the tree to extended family which came to visit during the next few weeks. Most importantly, we had all enjoyed a time of true reflection and growing gratitude toward the Lord who provided every good and perfect gift!

Songs of Thanksgiving

Singing is one of the ways that we are instructed to praise the Lord. Thanksgiving Hymns are an easy opportunity to glorify God before our families. Familiar even to unbelieving family members, music sometimes reaches folks' hearts in a way our words do not. We've seen family who resisted our hymn singing at first, finish with tears running down their faces. My grandfather said, "It reminds me of evenings singing as a family when I was a boy."

What did the Pilgrims sing?

At the time of their crossing, most of the English-speaking Protestant churches did not sing hymns, which they criticized as "songs of human invention," in formal worship, but preferred metrical or poetic versions of the Psalms or other passages of Scripture.

The Pilgrims brought copies of a psalter compiled by Henry Ainsworth, a fellow Separatist who saw his collection published in Amsterdam in 1612.

One that they might have sung as well is **"All People That On Earth Do Dwell,"** a metrical version of Psalm 100, sung to the same melody used for the Doxology (Words: William Kethe. Music: Louis Bourgeois. In *Fourscore and Seven Psalms of David* (Geneva, Switzerland: 1561)

> All people that on earth do dwell,
> Sing to the Lord with cheerful voice.
> Him serve with fear, His praise forth tell;
> Come ye before Him and rejoice.

The Lord, ye know, is God indeed;
Without our aid He did us make;
We are His folk, He doth us feed,
And for His sheep He doth us take.

O enter then His gates with praise;
Approach with joy His courts unto;
Praise, laud, and bless His Name always,
For it is seemly so to do.

For why? the Lord our God is good;
His mercy is for ever sure;
His truth at all times firmly stood,
And shall from age to age endure.

To Father, Son and Holy Ghost,
The God Whom Heaven and earth adore,
From men and from the angel host
Be praise and glory evermore.

We have our own favorites, too—one of which the Pilgrims may have heard during their time in Holland!

"We Gather Together To Ask The Lord's Blessing" is a Dutch hymn written in 1597 by Adrianus Valerius to celebrate a victory in the war for independence from Spain. Under the harsh rule of the Spanish Duke of Alva, the Reformed people of the Netherlands were not even allowed to meet to worship, even though the Reformation had swept the country and the majority of the populace were protestant, so "We Gather Together" is a song full of meaning.

The Relief of the Siege of Leiden

The Spanish crown tried to force the Dutch people to return to Catholicism and the rule of Spain at the point of the sword. It was a terrible war for the people: the Spanish Generals were treacherous, promising the lives of the inhabitants of cities who surrendered, then slaying men, women and children alike, saying that there was no need to keep your word to what they considered heretics. This gives a new poignancy to "The wicked oppressing, now cease from distressing."

This song was almost certainly sung among Christians throughout Holland during the time that the Pilgrims sojourned there. They had fled England, where they were persecuted for their faith, to live in the Netherlands, which had won not only their independence during the Eighty Years War, but freedom of religion. The Pilgrims dwelt in Leiden from 1608-9 until, concerned they were losing their children to the worldliness of those around them and desiring to take the gospel to the world, they left for the New World in 1620. This is a song the Pilgrims might have sung as they went about their work.

The English words by Theodore Baker are not a direct translation from the Dutch—they were translated first into Latin, then German, and finally English—, but the spirit of praise and gratefulness is the same. Listen on Hymnary: my.hymnary.org/song/170/we-gather-together

> We gather together to ask the Lord's blessing;
> He chastens and hastens His will to make known.
> The wicked oppressing now cease from distressing.
> Sing praises to His Name; He forgets not His own.
>
> Beside us to guide us, our God with us joining,
> Ordaining, maintaining His kingdom divine;
> So from the beginning the fight we were winning;
> Thou, Lord, were at our side, all glory be Thine!
>
> We all do extol Thee, Thou Leader triumphant,
> And pray that Thou still our Defender will be.
> Let Thy congregation escape tribulation;
> Thy Name be ever praised! O Lord, make us free!

"Come Ye Thankful People Come" is a song of the final harvest written in 1844 by the English clergyman Henry Alford. The interesting thing about this song, is that it takes the harvest celebration and turns our hearts to the final harvest of souls. Just as the landowner works diligently to bring in the harvest before winter comes, the Lord tells us to look on the fields that are white unto the harvest and to share His gospel with the world. There is so much truth in this song to share with your children!

Come, ye thankful people, come, raise the song of harvest home;
All is safely gathered in, ere the winter storms begin.
God our Maker doth provide for our wants to be supplied;
Come to God's own temple, come, raise the song of harvest home.

All the world is God's own field, fruit unto His praise to yield;
Wheat and tares together sown unto joy or sorrow grown.
First the blade and then the ear, then the full corn shall appear;
Lord of harvest, grant that we wholesome grain and pure may be.

For the Lord our God shall come, and shall take His harvest home;
From His field shall in that day all offenses purge away,
Giving angels charge at last in the fire the tares to cast;
But the fruitful ears to store in His garner evermore.

Even so, Lord, quickly come, bring Thy final harvest home;
Gather Thou Thy people in, free from sorrow, free from sin,
There, forever purified, in Thy garner to abide;
Come, with all Thine angels come, raise the glorious harvest home.

Listen on Hymnary: https://my.hymnary.org/song/104/come-ye-thankful-people-come

"**Now Thank We All Our God**" is a German hymn written by a Lutheran pastor, Martin Rinkhart, to celebrate deliverance during the Thirty Years' War (1618-1648). During the conflict, some areas of Germany lost more than a quarter of their population. Rinkhart's own town was overrun by the fighting on several occasions and suffered siege, famine, and epidemic among the religious and military refugees who gathered there—many of them in Rinkhart's own home. Finally, he was the only pastor spared, and conducted as many as fifty funerals in a single day. The hymn is rich with praise for the Trinity, thanks for God's blessings in the present, and a confident hope of glory in eternity!

> Now thank we all our God, with heart and hands and voices,
> Who wondrous things has done, in Whom this world rejoices;
> Who from our mothers' arms has blessed us on our way
> With countless gifts of love, and still is ours today.
>
> O may this bounteous God through all our life be near us,
> With ever joyful hearts and blessèd peace to cheer us;
> And keep us in His grace, and guide us when perplexed;
> And free us from all ills, in this world and the next!
>
> All praise and thanks to God the Father now be given;
> The Son and Him Who reigns with Them in highest Heaven;
> The one eternal God, whom earth and Heaven adore;
> For thus it was, is now, and shall be evermore.

Listen on Hymnary: https://my.hymnary.org/song/20/now-thank-we-all-our-god

The Thanksgiving Feast Menu

Roast Turkey
Fresh Cranberry Sauce
Cranberry Relish
Savory Turkey Gravy
Cornbread Dressing
Rice or Creamed Potatoes
Seven Layer Salad
Congealed Salad
Macaroni and Cheese Pie
Sweet Potato Soufflé
Green Bean Casserole
Garden Vegetables
Homemade Buttermilk Biscuits
Chocolate Meringue Pie
Pumpkin Cheesecake Pie

Becoming a Great Cook

Notes on These Recipes

The recipes in this book are designed to feed 12-14 people with some leftovers to enjoy. Please adjust as you need to.

If you don't fancy yourself a great cook, you might be a little alarmed when you glance over these recipes. Some don't include exact measurements. Others include a paragraph of explanation instead of a step-by-step formula. Don't let this concern you! These recipes can help you learn how to be more than just a cookbook-follower, but to become a creative force in your own kitchen! Here are a few tips to unleash the cook within:

Taste Everything

The best way to tell if the seasoning is right is to just taste it. If it tastes great uncooked (don't do this with meat, of course), it's going to taste incredible when it's done.

You Can Always Add More, But

The only way to take an excess out is to double or triple your recipe!

None of us will ever forget the epic time one of our boys was making Shepherd's Pie with instant potato flakes and added too much salt to the potatoes. He didn't taste them (How odd, he must have been under the weather!), and didn't realize it until he'd spread them over the meat. At that point, it was too late to double or triple the batch to save them – the filling was stuck to them. We dumped it all into a pot and added milk and water until the saltiness normalized. It made a wonderful lunch – Shepherd's Soup – that has been remembered with fondness ever since. Mistakes don't always turn out so felicitous, so, if you're not sure, add a little, taste it, then add more. And,

Turn Mistakes into New Recipes

Once I was making Blueberry Muffins when halfway through the recipe, I realized we were out of eggs! I was too frugal to throw away what I'd mixed together and too tired to go buy eggs, so I spread the thick mixture in a pan and baked it anyway.

It made the most incredible Blueberry Scones! I've been famous for them ever since...

Suit Your Family

The cookbook, *Mennonite Country Cooking,* given to me by my dear friend Carolyn, is one of my favorites. I was browsing in it one day when my eyes alighted on a delicious sounding recipe: Apple Dapple Cake. Only, it had nuts in it and I really don't care for nuts in cake. "Oh well, I'll just leave them out!" I thought. I considered that would leave fewer solids in the cake, so I decided to add more apples, but not quite as much as the nuts since apples soften and moisten in cooking. That adaptation has become one of our most favored recipes ever! Don't ever be afraid to adapt these recipes or any other to suit your family. Don't like vanilla extract? Try almond. Don't like garlic? Leave it out. Make it yours.

How to Roast a Turkey

About this time of year, you start seeing advertisements for "easy, no baste" turkeys and ways of preparing them. Funny though, the advertisements never show the pale, limp products of cooking a turkey in a plastic bag. Instead they always show brown, lovely roasted birds.

I first learned to cook a turkey when as a newlywed our first Thanksgiving, I turned to my favorite new cookbook, *The Joy of Cooking*. I loved it because it didn't just have recipes, but it taught me *how* to cook new things; the principles behind the processes.

This new (old) way was a bit more complicated, but was so much better, we've never been tempted to go back to foil or plastic bags. Sealing a turkey up in foil or plastic merely boils all the flavor out of it, like the difference between boiled chicken breasts and grilled ones. If you've never had a truly roasted turkey, you haven't eaten turkey! Imagine turkey so delicious the juices run out as you cook it and so tender a fork slices right through it. You've got to try it!

Gather ahead of time:

A turkey
> I buy the largest I can find, frozen, because it is so much cheaper, and put it in the fridge in its package in a plastic bag to catch leakage five days in advance.

Cotton fabric
> Buy white or natural muslin or plain cotton fabric in a square large enough to cover the top of the turkey. A large, clean man's handkerchief will work in a pinch. Don't plan to use this for anything again!

Needle and any neutral color sturdy thread – white, beige, brown, etc.
Marinade and injector, if you are Cajun
A large shallow pan with sides an inch or two deep, a rack is nice
Real butter, a couple of sticks
Chicken stock, a couple of cans
A baster makes this much easier
A bowl to put the drippings
A meat thermometer to tell when it's done

First, figure out how early you need to start your turkey. I recommend subtracting one hour from the time you want to eat, then allowing 15 minutes per pound for a large bird. So, if we wanted to eat at a 20 pound bird at 1pm, we'd subtract one hour to get to noon, then subtract 15 x 20 = 5 hours. That means the turkey would need to be put in the oven at 7am.

Allow about 30 minutes to prep the turkey. Set the butter out to soften. And turn the oven on to 450 degrees or so. Clean your sink well with soap, and put the turkey in it. Remove and discard the plastic packaging and rinse the turkey with cool water. Look in the cavities at both ends and remove the neck and bag of giblets. If they are frozen stuck, rinse with slightly warm water until you can pull them out. If the turkey is trussed with plastic, remove it with a knife or scissors.

Grasp the end of a wing and carefully bend it down under the bird so the turkey is sort of leaning on its forearms. Repeat with the other wing. This makes for a much prettier cooked bird than with the wings sticking up.

Use the needle and thread to sew up the openings in the turkey. This will make it much prettier on the table and keep it juicy while cooking. It doesn't have to be neat – the stitches will fade into the brown of the skin as it cooks. Just start at the top of the split, gently stretch the skin together and stitch it together.

This is the time to inject marinade if you have to have it spicy like our Cajun friends, or if you'd like to try that for a change. Inject deeply into the breast and thighs in several places.

Rub butter all over the turkey and place in the pan – elbows down – it will rest on its wings. It's best for the bird to rest on a rack, so the bottom part doesn't get soggy, but if you don't have one, just pull out the drippings often.

Place the turkey in the oven and immediately turn down to 350, or perhaps 325 for a very large bird you're not in a hurry for.

Melt the rest of the butter in the microwave and submerge the fabric square until pretty well soaked.

After 30 minutes cooking, pull out the turkey, baste with butter and cover with the fabric, tucking any edges in the pan.

Baste every 15 to 20 minutes. Baste with the remaining butter until it is gone, then baste with chicken broth until you have enough pan drippings to use those. Use chicken broth freely, it'll give you more drippings, which means more gravy, in the end.

Baste under and over the fabric very generously. If the fabric gets dried out, take out and submerge in broth or drippings.

If you forget and miss a basting, don't worry about it; just baste whenever you remember it. The more you baste, the better it will be, but no matter how many times you forget, it will still be better than any turkey you've ever had.

While the turkey is cooking, if you like lots of gravy, cover the neck and giblets with water and simmer to make more broth.

Cook until your thermometer reads 180 degrees Fahrenheit and has been checked in several places. It'll look gorgeously brown and perfectly done at this point. Totally ignore the little pop up thingy – it sometimes won't pop up until the turkey is hopelessly dried out.

Pull the turkey out of the oven and set aside for at least 30 minutes to firm up before carving. Now is the time to cook the rolls, finish up any casseroles you need to and to make the gravy out of the drippings.

Bring to the table whole, on a platter with a carving knife. It's too pretty to carve in the kitchen!

Start carving by removing the drumsticks and thighs, then slicing deeply across at the bottom of the breast meat. Then slice vertically to make lovely slices to pass around for the feast. Be sure to slice up a thigh and drumstick for those that enjoy dark meat.

When the feast is done, do not discard the carcass – you'll be missing a treat! Instead, carve all the meat that is easily removed for leftovers, turkey salad and other deliciousness. Then push the carcass down into a large stockpot, cover with water and simmer until the meat falls off and the bones separate. Then let cool, put in the fridge and make gumbo in a day or two.

Next Day Turkey Gumbo

Remove cool turkey stock pot. Spoon off the solid fat, then remove the bones and gristle. Heat the broth and taste – add a little water if too strong, but it's probably not. Add a little chicken broth or boil down if it is too weak.

Add sliced okra, if you love it like I do, and you can find some in November. Cook until tender.

Dice peppers and onions (and celery, if you care for it) and sauté in butter, then add to gumbo.

Add salt until it tastes wonderful, not bland. I suspect it will take a teaspoon or two.

Add black pepper and/or Tony Chachere's Creole Seasoning until almost as spicy as you can enjoy.

Serve over hot rice in a bowl for a delicious lunch. Saltines or garlic bread are a nice accompaniment.

Cornbread Dressing

Leftover Cornbread, don't panic, ideas below
Leftover Biscuits, don't panic, ideas below
Onion or two, diced
3 or 4 T real butter
Dried sage, lots.
Chicken broth, 2 or more cans
Eggs, about three

Crumble equal amounts of cornbread and biscuits into your casserole dish until almost full but with room to stir it still. Saute onion in butter and stir into bread mixture. Add dried sage to bread mixture to taste. It is most accurate to do this while bread is still dry. It should be pretty sage-y.

Pour chicken broth over bread mixture until it is thoroughly dampened but doesn't have broth in the bottom. Beat eggs in bowl, add some salt and pepper. Pour over dressing. This will hold it together nicely.

Bake at 350 degrees until solid and beginning to brown. This takes from 45 minutes to an hour or more depending on the depth of the dish.

Cornbread, use any your family likes. You can even use two boxes of Jiffy cornbread mix, but cook it in an iron skillet heated in the oven with oil in the bottom so it's nice and crusty.

Biscuits, any standard recipe will do, one using 2-3 cups flour will be about the right amount. Don't use "whop biscuits" as we call canned ones, as they get soggy too easily. Better to buy some from Bojangles or KFC.

Grandma's Cranberry Relish

1 12 oz bag of fresh cranberries
1 navel orange, do NOT peel
1 cup sugar

Quarter the orange. Process all ingredients in a food processor or blender until minced, but not pureed. May be done in batches. Store in fridge. Serve cold. Incredibly fresh and delicious tasting!

To Can: Sterilize jars in boiling water in water bath canner for ten minutes. Preheat lids in water on medium. Heat relish in a thick-bottomed saucepan on medium until hot. Drain jars and fill with hot relish leaving ½ inch air space. Clean rims with a wet paper towel. Add lids, then bands. Screw down but do not tighten. Use a jar lifter to gently place jars back in hot water in canner. Replace the lid. Heat over high heat until vigorously boiling and process for ten minutes. Turn off heat and let sit for five minutes. Remove jars with jar lifter and set on towel on counter. Do not disturb for 12-24 hours. Processing times are from "Cranberry Orange Chutney" in the USDA Complete Guide to Home Canning, Guide 2: Selecting, Preparing, and Canning Fruit and Fruit Products.

Fresh Cranberry Sauce

1 12oz bag fresh cranberries
1 cup sugar
2 T cornstarch (T = tablespoonfuls)
1/3 cup orange juice or water

Mix cornstarch and sugar in a saucepan, add liquid and cranberries.

Cook on medium until it bubbles merrily. Turn down to simmer and cook until begins to thicken nicely. Stir until cranberries are as broken up as you like. Remove from heat, cool, and refrigerate covered until ready to eat. Serve in a pretty dish with a small spoon to serve with.

Savory Turkey Gravy

Turkey drippings, use spoon or use baster to remove top light colored fat layer, then measure.
Real salted butter, two to three tablespoonfuls per cup of drippings
Plain flour, two to three tablespoonfuls per cup of drippings

In a large frying pan, preferably iron, melt two to three tablespoonfuls (more for thicker gravy) of real salted butter per cup of drippings or stock you want to make into gravy.

Add two to three tablespoonsful of flour per cup of drippings and stir into a light paste. If this becomes a thick paste, add more butter.

Stir the roux (that's the flour and butter mixture) and cook on medium to medium low until the roux turns light brown.

Slowly add broth while stirring madly to prevent lumps. Turn down and simmer until the thickness you like.

Pour into a gravy boat and serve with a ladle. A bowl and spoon can also be used.

Creamed or Mashed Potatoes

Potatoes, washed and peeled, if you like, about a medium size potato per person, two for teen males.
One large turnip, washed and peeled, to give it an excellent flavor
Milk or cream
Real butter

Place potatoes and turnip in a large pot and cover with water. Turn stove on high until boiling, then turn down to medium to medium high so that water doesn't boil too wildly and splash out.

When potatoes pierce easily with a fork, when they are tender, drain out water. Add about half a stick of butter or more for a large pot of potatoes and beat with a mixer. Add cream (for richer taste), evaporated milk, or milk until it mixes freely and is just the texture you like. Add salt to taste, and white pepper if you like. Cover until serving time, then stir before serving.

Rice

To make each 3 cups of rice, use:
1 cup dry rice, long grain for more separate rice, short grain for stickier
2 cups water

In a large saucepan or stockpot, boil measured amount of water. Add dry rice in proportions above. Place on stove and heat on high until mixture boils, turn down to one notch above low and cover.

Cover tightly and cook for 20 minutes. Stay out of it! The steam cooks the rice and if you let the steam out... When done, remove from heat, fluff with fork and add butter.

Seven Layer Salad

Lettuce, iceberg, bibb, romaine or other firm lettuce, washed and torn, large head or two to three hearts of romaine
English or green peas, cooked firm and cooled, a cup or two
Mild onion, Vidalia or red, diced, one
Bell pepper, green, yellow or red, diced, one
Grated cheddar cheese, sharp preferably, or other favorite or strong cheese, 2 cups or more
Salad-dressing type mayonnaise, a cup or more
Brown sugar, 2-3 tablespoons
Bacon, browned, cooled, and crumbled, at least 3 or 4 slices, up to a pound

Layer one third of lettuce in bottom of casserole dish, we use a 9"x13" one. Sprinkle a third of the peas, onions and peppers on top, one at a time. Repeat twice.

Carefully spread salad-dressing type mayonnaise across top of mixture, being very sure to completely cover all the way to the edges. This will keep the vegetables crisp and delicious. Sprinkle brown sugar lightly across the top, then add bacon crumbles. Cover tightly and refrigerate until serving. This can be made the night before.

This can be varied with hard-boiled eggs, green onions, grated carrot, raisins, sweetened, dried cranberries, broccoli or cauliflower.

Orange Congealed Salad

2 small boxes apricot gelatin, peach or orange may be used in a pinch
16 oz or so, cottage cheese, whole milk type is extra creamy
16 oz frozen whipped topping, thawed or 16 oz whipped cream
Large can mandarin oranges, about 16oz, drained.

Mix dry jello mix into cottage cheese until thoroughly wetted. Stir in mandarin oranges, then fold in whipped cream or topping. Cover and refrigerate until ready to serve. So delicious!

Real Southern Macaroni & Cheese Pie

3 cups dry small elbow macaroni
1 - 2 lb extra sharp cheese, grated, the sharper the better
3-4 cups milk
4 eggs, beaten
1 teaspoon salt
¼ to ½ teaspoon pepper
Butter, to dot

Boil macaroni for 10 minutes, drain. It should be cooked, but firm.

Layer cheese with macaroni in a deep casserole – this will fill a 9x13 or a little more. Start with macaroni, add more cheese than you think you need, and end with cheese. Stop and refrigerate at this point if you'd like to cook it the next day.

Beat eggs in bottom of 4 cup measure or quart bowl. Add milk to 4 cup mark. Add salt and pepper. Pour through macaroni. Liquid should rise an inch or two in pan, feel free to add more or less.

Dot with butter and cook at 350 until solid (no white liquid runs when you tilt it) and beginning to get crispy on the corners. Should take about an hour.

My grandmother, Mama Helen, had a cook, Nanny, who was famous for this dish. We children were sent into the kitchen to spy out the recipe since Nanny didn't allow adults in her kitchen and didn't share recipes. It's still that good! Hal's Granny was also known for macaroni and cheese. Hal says mine tastes just like hers.

Note: This recipe may be called macaroni and cheese, macaroni and cheese pie or macaroni and cheese soufflé, but may *never* be called mac and cheese. That's something entirely different that comes in a box or is made from scratch, but in a pot.

Sweet Potato Souffle

About 5-6 large sweet potatoes (large is a relative term, you want about 5 cups mashed)
½ stick butter (1/4 cup)
¾-1 cup brown sugar (taste and add more if you like it sweeter)
3 eggs
1 teaspoon vanilla
½ cup orange juice, cream, evaporated milk or milk
½ teaspoon salt
1 teaspoon cinnamon
½ teaspoon nutmeg
½ cup raisins, regular or golden
Bag of marshmallows or pecans and a crumble of butter, brown sugar, and oats

Peel and boil sweet potatoes until soft. Drain and Immediately add butter. Add liquid and mash with beaters. Add eggs and seasonings. Stir in raisins. Spread in a casserole dish. Stop at this point if you'd like to prepare ahead and refrigerate. Heat at 350 degrees until piping hot. Takes about 30-45 minutes, depending on starting temperature. Remove from the oven and put marshmallows on top. Return to oven (on broil if you need them quickly) and cook until marshmallows begin to brown on top. Keep an eye on them! Serve hot.

Green Bean Casserole

4 cans French-cut green beans, drained
2 cans cream of mushroom soup
1 Tablespoon Worcestershire sauce
1 clove garlic, minced, or ½ teaspoon pre-minced
1 ½ cups French-fried onion rings
1 small can mushrooms, optional

In casserole dish, mix soup, Worcestershire and seasonings. Stir in green beans and 1/3 of the onions. Spread out evenly. Stop at this point if you are cooking ahead and refrigerate. Bake at 350 degrees until warm, about 30 minutes. Sprinkle remaining onions on top and return to oven until piping hot and onions are beginning to brown.

Garden Vegetables

We usually have collards, cooked well in advance, but any green vegetable will add color and variety to your feast. For most vegetables, place in a pot with an inch of water in the bottom. Bring the water to a boil, cover and turn down to simmer until desired tenderness. Collards require more strenuous preparation, washing extremely thoroughly, chopping, then cooking for a long period of time with pork for seasoning in a slow cooker or a bit less time in an electric pressure cooker. Be patient and cook until they are actually tender!

Homemade Buttermilk Biscuits

This recipe has won several blue ribbons at the North Carolina State Fair!

3 1/2 cups white self-rising flour, a Southern brand is best because it has less gluten and will be more tender and light. (If you can't find self-rising, add 2 teaspoons salt and 4 teaspoons baking powder.)
1 teaspoon sugar
1/2 teaspoon baking soda
5 Tablespoons butter
2/3 to 3/4 cup buttermilk

Preheat oven to 450. Make sure butter is ice cold. Mix dry ingredients in a large bowl.

Cut in butter or (I like this better for a more consistent result) use a cheese grater to grate the butter into the dry ingredients. Coat cheese grater with flour mixture, then grate on the larger side quickly, making sure not to let it jam up in the grater, but stopping to toss it lightly in the flour every so often. Do NOT overstir. The butter should remain in grated pieces for flakiness.

Add buttermilk until dough is moistened. Do not over-stir. Dust flour on a clean board. Turn out dough and knead lightly JUST until the dough comes together, like two or three times max. Do not over-handle. Pat the dough into the thickness you want. I usually go for an inch thick or even a little more. Cut with a flour-dusted biscuit cutter, pushing it straight down and pulling straight up, never twisting. Twisting the cutter will limit the rise of your biscuits. Lift onto a cookie sheet. Bake immediately or set aside for not more than an hour or so until ready to bake.

Bake at 450 degrees until turning light brown on the tops and bottom, but still pale on the sides.

Chocolate Meringue Pie

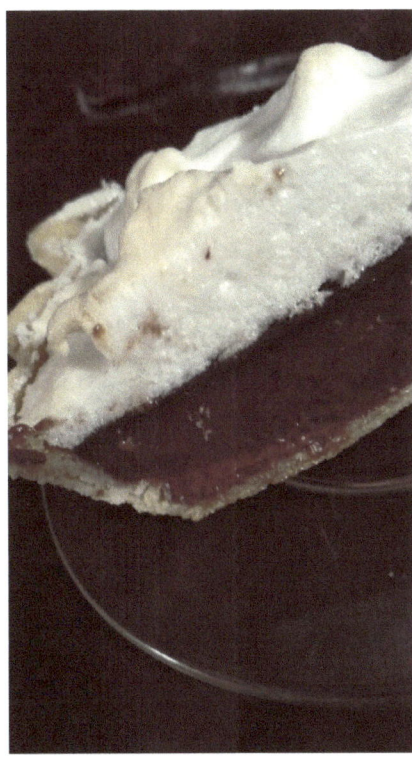

2 large 5 oz boxes Jello Cook and Serve Pudding and Pie Filling, Chocolate
6 cups whole milk
2 single pie crusts, If I buy them, I prefer the rolled kind found in the refrigerated section of the store
4 eggs, separated, at room temperature, with no yolk in the whites at all
Pinch of cream of tartar, optional, but helps
6 Tablespoons sugar
1 teaspoon vanilla extract
2 pie pans, glass is prettiest

This is a simple recipe using many bought ingredients, but it is just exactly the one I grew to love growing up. I can make it from scratch now, but why not do something easy when you are already so busy?

Cook the pudding mix in a saucepan according to the directions.

While it is heating, roll out the dough and lift into the pans. Trim the edges at the edge of the pan. An easy pretty edge can be made by putting your two index fingers just a thumbwidth apart on the edge, then using your thumb between them to poke the edge up there slightly to one side. Continue around to make a pretty scalloped edge. Prick the bottom and bake at 350 until just beginning to brown.

When the pudding is boiling briskly and thickening, beat the egg yolks and add just a small spoonful of pudding and stir it into the eggs. Add a little larger spoonful of pudding and stir in. This warms the eggs gradually and will keep them from scrambling as you put them in the pudding. Once it's about half and half eggs and pudding, add the eggs to the pudding and stir in. Take the pudding off the heat and stir a time or two and pour into the pie crusts. Set aside.

In a perfectly clean bowl and using completely clean mixer paddles, begin beating the egg whites. When frothy, add the cream of tartar. This stabilizes the egg whites and makes it easy to produce a nice meringue.

Beat until almost stiff, then slowly add the sugar, beating all the time.

Add vanilla while continuing to beat. Stop when the peaks stand up and just the end droops down.

Spread meringue over the hot pies, being very sure indeed to cover every inch of the filling and touch the pastry on every side. This helps keep the meringue from shrinking in the fridge.

Bake the pie at 350 degrees until the meringue begins to brown prettily on the peaks, but is still a lovely light brown. Refrigerate until serving. Makes two pies.

Pumpkin Cheesecake Pie

Cheesecake Layer
16oz cream cheese, room temperature
2 egg
1/2 cup sugar
2 teaspoon vanilla

Pumpkin Layer
2 ½ cups pumpkin, cooked and mashed or canned
1 cup sugar
2 teaspoon cinnamon
½ teaspoon nutmeg
½ teaspoon ginger (or substitute 1 tablespoon pumpkin pie spice for these three spices)
Pinch of salt
4 eggs

2 cups of evaporated milk or whole milk

2 single unbaked pie crusts, If I buy them, I like the rolled ones in the refrigerated section of the store
2 pie pans
Maple syrup, a couple of tablespoons
16 pecan halves

Roll out the dough and lift into the pans. Trim the edges at the edge of the pan. An easy pretty edge can be made by putting your two index fingers just a thumbwidth apart on the edge, then using your thumb between them to poke the edge up there slightly to one side. Continue around to make a pretty scalloped edge.

Beat cream cheese, sugar and vanilla until fluffy. Add eggs one at a time, beating well after each addition. This will turn out much nicer if cream cheese is truly room temperature. Spread into the bottom of the two pie crusts and place in fridge while you prepare pumpkin so it firms up.

In the same bowl, without washing (you don't need any more dishes to wash today), place pumpkin, sugar and seasonings and beat well. Add eggs one at a time, beating after each addition. Add milk slowly while beating. Holding bowl just above the cheese mixture, gently pour over cream cheese until almost but not quite to the top of the pie pan.

Bake at 350 degrees until firm, about 70 minutes. Spread a little maple syrup over the top with the back of your spoon. It adds a lovely sheen. Arrange the pecans on the top. I place two on each slice just touching at the ends, like leaves. Refrigerate until serving. Makes two pies.

The ingredient list for this pie recipe has been published in numerous places. The earliest I can find was in the November 1975 edition of *The Workbasket Magazine,* but I have no idea if this is the original. Ingredient lists may not be copyrighted, but we'd love to give credit where due. The instructions are my own.

The Shopping List

The list of everything you need to make the recipes included here. Mark off things already in your cabinet and you are ready to go!

A turkey
> I buy the largest I can find, frozen, because it is so much cheaper, and put it in the fridge in its package in a plastic bag to catch leakage five days in advance. Turkeys are more cost effective the bigger they are!

Cotton fabric
> Buy white or natural muslin or plain cotton fabric in a square large enough to cover the top of the turkey. A large, clean man's handkerchief will work nicely in a pinch. Don't plan to use this for anything again!

Needle and any neutral color sturdy thread – white, beige, brown, etc.
A meat thermometer to tell when it's done, if you don't have one
A turkey baster, if you don't have one

Marinade and injector, if you are Cajun, or eat like they do!
Salt & Pepper
Tony Chachere's Creole Seasoning for the gumbo
Dried sage, lots
2 T cornstarch
4 teaspoon vanilla
3 teaspoon cinnamon
1 teaspoon nutmeg
½ teaspoon ginger
2 Tablespoons baking powder
1 clove garlic, minced, or ½ teaspoon pre-minced
Salad-dressing type mayonnaise, a cup or more
Pinch of cream of tartar, optional, but helps

Real butter, 2 1/2lb
Eggs, 20
Milk, 10 cup
Buttermilk, 2 cups
16oz cream cheese, room temperature
Orange juice, 1 cup, optional or water
Extra sharp cheddar cheese, 2-2 ½ lb or more

16 oz or so, cottage cheese, whole milk type is extra creamy
4 single pie crusts, if I buy them, I prefer the rolled kind in the refrigerated section
Bacon, browned, cooled, and crumbled, at least 3 or 4 slices, up to a pound

Chicken stock, 4 cans
Large can mandarin oranges, about 16oz
4 cans French-cut green beans
2 cans cream of mushroom soup
1 Tablespoon Worcestershire sauce
1 ½ cups French-fried onion rings
1 small can mushrooms, optional
2 ½ cups pumpkin

Okra, if you want it in your gumbo
Bell peppers, 2
Onions, 5 (one must be mild like Vidalia)
1 - 12oz bag fresh cranberries
Potatoes, about a medium size potato per person, two for teen males.
One large turnip, washed and peeled, to give it an excellent flavor
Lettuce, iceberg, bibb, romaine or other firm lettuce, large head or 2-3 romaine hearts
Navel Orange, 1
About 5-6 large sweet potatoes
Garden vegetables, 2-3 lb, fresh or frozen

Rice, 2lb for gumbo, 2lb for feast, if you use it
Plain flour, 1 cup, plus 2 to make biscuits for leftovers, plus 4 for biscuits
Leftover Cornbread, or ingredients to make it
Leftover Biscuits, or ingredients to make it
3 cup sugar
3 cups dry small elbow macaroni
Brown sugar, 1 c plus 2-3 tablespoons
2 small boxes apricot gelatin, peach or orange may be used in a pinch
Bag large marshmallows
2 large 5 oz boxes Jello Cook and Serve Pudding and Pie Filling, Chocolate
16 Pecan Halves
½ cup raisins, regular or golden

English or green peas, frozen or fresh, ½ lb
16oz frozen whipped topping, thawed or 16oz whipped cream

Cooking Schedule

In Advance

Task	√
Put turkey in fridge to defrost (this can take 5-6 days in a huge bird)	
Do your shopping! See shopping list.	
Cook bacon for Seven Layer Salad	
Cook or purchase biscuits for Dressing	
Cook cornbread for Dressing	
Make Cranberry Sauce, refrigerate	

Tuesday and Wednesday before Thanksgiving

Task	√
Boil macaroni	
Layer Macaroni and Cheese, do not add eggs and milk, refrigerate	
Boil sweet potatoes	
Assemble Sweet Potato Souffle, refrigerate	
Assemble Green Bean Casserole, don't put onions on top, refrigerate	
Saute onions for dressing	
Assemble and season cornbread dressing, refrigerate	
Chop Veggies for Seven Layer Salad	
Assemble Congealed Salad and Cranberry Relish	
Bake pie shell for Chocolate Pudding Pie	
Cook pudding for Chocolate Pudding Pie	
Make meringue for Chocolate Pudding Pie	
Assemble Chocolate Pudding Pie and toast meringue, refrigerate	
Make Pumpkin Cheesecake Pie	
Wash, chop and prepare any Garden Vegetables for steaming tomorrow	

Blanks of these forms are in the back of the book for you to adapt to your own use.

Thanksgiving Day

Hrs before Serving	Task	√
As calculated	Preheat oven to 450° and prepare turkey for oven	
	Turn oven down to 350° and put turkey in	
	Make breakfast	
	Baste turkey as often as you remember	
	Set the table	
	Sit down for a few minutes and relax	
	Gather reading and hymns for celebration (or better yet, have the children do it)	
2-3 hours	Boil potatoes if you are having Creamed Potatoes	
	Pour eggs and milk in Macaroni and Cheese	
2 hours	Place Macaroni and Cheese and Cornbread Dressing in the oven	
	Make biscuits and set aside on pan to bake later (and if you don't mind them not being hot out of the oven, you can cook them earlier)	
1 ½ hours	Put Green Bean Casserole and Sweet Potato Souffle in the oven as space opens up, cover casseroles with foil as they come out to keep them warm	
	Gather children, tell them to get washed up and get them helping checking the table, welcoming guests, and getting drinks ready	
1 hour	Remove turkey as it reaches 180°, remove drippings and set aside	
	Make Turkey Gravy	
	Steam Vegetables as Needed	
	Have children put salt & pepper, butter on the table.	
½ hour-1 hour	Top Green Bean Casserole with onions and Sweet Potato Souffle with marshmallows and toast them both	
	Bake Biscuits	
	Transfer Turkey to platter. If carving turkey in the kitchen, have husband do that	

	Have children put Cranberry Sauce and Relish, Seven Layer Salad, Congealed Salad, serving spoons, and drinks on the table,	
	Pour Gravy in serving dish, put Vegetables in Dish.	
	Wash your hands, take off your apron and call everyone to the Feast	

The Feast

An Order of Events

Place five kernels of corn (using kernels from an ear of Indian corn is a nice touch) on each unserved plate.

The Master of the Feast, usually Dad, should welcome everyone to the Thanksgiving Feast. He could say,

"Welcome to our Feast of Thanksgiving. Nearly four hundred years ago, our Pilgrim forefathers gathered to thank the Lord for bringing them through the very difficult first year of the Plymouth settlement. Starvation and disease had swept away nearly half their number, but the famine had passed and plenty had finally come to the Colony. Some 90 members of the Wampanoag tribe joined them in their celebration which included feasting, games and races."

The Master then calls on one of the children and says (if you choose to place five kernels of corn on each plate), "_____ will explain the kernels of corn on your plate." The child reads the poem "Five Kernels of Corn".

The Master of the Feast explains, "We'd be grateful if during the meal you'd try to share one thing for which you are thankful for each of the kernels of corn you received."

The Master than says, "Let us pray," and in his prayer, thanks God not only for the food that has been served, but for all the blessings of the proceeding year.

After he says, "In Christ's name, Amen," he should say, "Please, be served!" with a big smile on his face.

After the meal, the Master of the Feast should say, "Thank you so much for joining us. We'd be grateful if you'd join us as well in a few hymns of Thanksgiving." This can take place at the table, in the living room before cleaning up, or after cleaning up dinner. It takes some nerve to do this, but it really pays off in testimony. There are song sheets to be printed at the end of this book. This is a great time for the children to put on a play or charade, too.

Songs of Thanksgiving Sheet

We Gather Together

We gather together to ask the Lord's blessing;
He chastens and hastens His will to make known.
The wicked oppressing now cease from distressing.
Sing praises to His Name; He forgets not His own.

Beside us to guide us, our God with us joining,
Ordaining, maintaining His kingdom divine;
So from the beginning the fight we were winning;
Thou, Lord, were at our side, all glory be Thine!

We all do extol Thee, Thou Leader triumphant,
And pray that Thou still our Defender will be.
Let Thy congregation escape tribulation;
Thy Name be ever praised! O Lord, make us free!

All People That On Earth Do Dwell

All people that on earth do dwell,
Sing to the Lord with cheerful voice.
Him serve with fear, His praise forth tell;
Come ye before Him and rejoice.

The Lord, ye know, is God indeed;
Without our aid He did us make;
We are His folk, He doth us feed,
And for His sheep He doth us take.

O enter then His gates with praise;
Approach with joy His courts unto;
Praise, laud, and bless His Name always,
For it is seemly so to do.

For why? the Lord our God is good;
His mercy is for ever sure;
His truth at all times firmly stood,
And shall from age to age endure.

To Father, Son and Holy Ghost,
The God Whom Heaven and earth adore,
From men and from the angel host
Be praise and glory evermore.

Now Thank We All Our God

Now thank we all our God, with heart and hands and voices,
Who wondrous things has done, in Whom this world rejoices;
Who from our mothers' arms has blessed us on our way
With countless gifts of love, and still is ours today.

O may this bounteous God through all our life be near us,
With ever joyful hearts and blessèd peace to cheer us;
And keep us in His grace, and guide us when perplexed;
And free us from all ills, in this world and the next!

All praise and thanks to God the Father now be given;
The Son and Him Who reigns with Them in highest Heaven;
The one eternal God, whom earth and Heaven adore;
For thus it was, is now, and shall be evermore.

Come, Ye Thankful People, Come

Come, ye thankful people, come, raise the song of harvest home;
All is safely gathered in, ere the winter storms begin.
God our Maker doth provide for our wants to be supplied;
Come to God's own temple, come, raise the song of harvest home.

All the world is God's own field, fruit unto His praise to yield;
Wheat and tares together sown unto joy or sorrow grown.
First the blade and then the ear, then the full corn shall appear;
Lord of harvest, grant that we wholesome grain and pure may be.

For the Lord our God shall come, and shall take His harvest home;
From His field shall in that day all offenses purge away,
Giving angels charge at last in the fire the tares to cast;
But the fruitful ears to store in His garner evermore.

Even so, Lord, quickly come, bring Thy final harvest home;
Gather Thou Thy people in, free from sorrow, free from sin,
There, forever purified, in Thy garner to abide;
Come, with all Thine angels come, raise the glorious harvest home.

Cooking Schedule

In Advance

Task	√

Tuesday and Wednesday before Thanksgiving

Task	√

Thanksgiving Day

Hrs before Serving	Task	√

Our Other Great Resources

Five books that will help you make the holidays
more Christ-centered,
more memorable,
and more fun
without more stress!

Available in Hard Copies or eBooks

**Get the bundle for $5 off with the coupon code
HOLIDAYFIVE**

at raisingrealmen.com/holidayfive

Love History? Did you know Theodore Roosevelt wrote a book for children?

He did. He wanted to teach virtue and character to boys and girls through American History. Hero Tales is the result!

And we've got it in AudioBook, complete with sound effects! Get it here:

RaisingRealMen.com/herotales

Got boys? Get Hope – the Christian Small Publishers' Book of the Year!

You are not alone! Join Hal & Melanie, parents of six sons (and two daughters) in the adventure of raising godly young men!

"Just what the doctor ordered…" – Parenting columnist John Rosemond, author of *Parenting by the Book*

"Raising Real Men is long overdue… this book is a breath of fresh air." - Dr. Tedd Tripp, Author, Shepherding a Child's Heart

"This is a book that every family should have…" – J. Michael Smith, Esq, President, HSLDA

Available in hard copy, audiobook, ebook, Kindle, and more! Order today at www.RaisingRealMen.com/orders

Have a preteen? Has your preteen ever climbed on an emotional rollercoaster and invited you to join them?

Don't get a ticket for that ride!

Instead, get real practical help with your tweens and preteens on topics like discipline and discipling, social anxiety, sibling conflict, media use and more.

"Literally the best non-fiction book I've ever read!" – Megan Knight, mother of tweens

Find out more at raisingrealmen.com/product/nolongerlittle/

Did you know we have all kinds of great character-building gifts for your children?

Have you read A Cry From Egypt in your history curriculum yet? Written and illustrated by homeschool graduates, it's now a part of Tapestry of Grace, Biblioplan for Families, and The Grand Story!

Now, it's available as Radio Theatre! Your family will love it – and be encouraged to believe in the historic truth of God's Word!

Can you teach your kids to be grateful while they're laughing their head off? Sure you can! Pollyanna's not preachy, or stuffy, or even Disneyfied. She's hilarious! And she'll make you all more grateful.

The Hilarious Attitude Changer!

And other classic audiobooks, too!

The subscription box that builds your skills! Craftsman Crate and Craftsman Crate Apprentice (for parents to use with students six to twelve) teaches artisanal craft skills using real tools in totally complete kits – no trips to the store.

Check out our other great resources for raising boys, struggling learners, homeschooling high school, biblical family life, making marriage great, communication and coping with the challenging preteen age!

Join our online community: RaisingRealMen.com – our blog and store

Find us everywhere on social media @raisingrealmen and @halandmelanie

Acknowledgements

All of our work flows out of the good gifts of God the Father, who sent His Son, Jesus Christ to pay the penalty for our sin. All glory is His alone. Every day is Thanksgiving for the redeemed.

We are grateful for our eight great children, who help us and bless us in so many ways. Thanks, guys!

We especially want to thank the many great cooks in our lives – Nana, Granny, Grand-Nana, Mama Helen, the original Granny, Grandma, Nanny, and all those who have influenced us. That influence is evident in these pages. Thank you!

Images

Embarkation of the Pilgrims, Robert Walter Weir, 1857
http://en.wikipedia.org/wiki/File:Brooklyn_Museum_-_Embarkation_of_the_Pilgrims_-_Robert_Walter_Weir_-_overall.jpg

The Mayflower Compact, 1620, Jean Leon Jerome Ferris, early 1900s
http://en.wikipedia.org/wiki/File:The_Mayflower_Compact_1620_cph.3g07155.jpg

The Old Fort and the First Meeting House, from *The Romantic Story of the Mayflower Pilgrims,* Albert Christopher Addison, 1911
http://www.histarch.uiuc.edu/plymouth/images/addison-024.GIF

The First Thanksgiving at Plymouth, Jennie A. Brownscombe, 1914

Autumn Gourds and Such, gun4hire, Stock Exchange photo
http://www.sxc.hu/browse.phtml?f=view&id=1106973

George Washington, Rembrandt Peale
http://en.wikipedia.org/wiki/File:Portrait_of_George_Washington.jpeg

Abraham Lincoln, George Peter Alexander Healy, 1869
http://en.wikipedia.org/wiki/File:AbrahamLincolnOilPainting1869Restored.jpg

Abraham Lincoln reading to his son, Tad
http://en.wikipedia.org/wiki/File:A%26TLincoln.jpg

Pilgrim, Gheorghe Tatterescu-Palerin, 19th Century
http://en.wikipedia.org/wiki/File:Gheorghe_Tattarescu_-_Pelerin.jpg

Relief of Leiden, Otto van Veen, 1574
http://en.wikipedia.org/wiki/File:Veen01.jpg

Front Page of the Bradford Journal
http://en.wikipedia.org/wiki/File:Of_Plimoth_Plantation_First_1900.jpg

Wheat Harvest on the Palouse, Idaho, USDA, before 2004
http://commons.wikimedia.org/wiki/File:Wheat_harvest.jpg

Bozogumbo, Jason Perlow, 2005
http://commons.wikimedia.org/wiki/File:Bozogumbo.jpg

Cooking Cranberries, Tracy, from North Brookfield, Massachusetts
http://en.wikipedia.org/wiki/File:Cooking_cranberries.jpg

Indian Corn, DontBblu, Stock Exchange photo, 2006
http://www.sxc.hu/browse.phtml?f=view&id=628194

Washington Resigns His Commission, John Turnbull, 1817
http://en.wikipedia.org/wiki/File:General_George_Washington_Resigning_his_Commission.jpg

Gustavus' Victory at Breitenfeld http://en.wikipedia.org/wiki/File:Thirtywar.gif

Pumpkin Patch 3, Naneki, Stock Exchange photo, 2011
http://www.sxc.hu/photo/1367968

Sweet Potato Casserole, Deposit Photos
https://depositphotos.com/photos/sweet-potato-casserole.html?qview=91861824

Green Bean Casserole, Deposit Photos https://depositphotos.com/photos/green-bean-casserole.html?filter=all&qview=619716080

Bowl of Rice, Deposit Photos https://depositphotos.com/photos/plain-rice-in-serving-bowl.html?filter=all&qview=267000950

All other images ©2006-2025 Hal & Melanie Young, All Rights Reserved

www.ingramcontent.com/pod-product-compliance
Lightning Source LLC
Chambersburg PA
CBHW050756110526
44588CB00002B/15